SIESTA KEY

THE BOOK

By Danny Stooksbury

SIESTA KEY: THE BOOK

Copyright © 2014 by Danny Stooksbury

Layout and design by Higher Level Publishing

Edited by Heather Rolls

All rights reserved. No part of this book may be reproduced in any form by any electronic or mechanical means including photocopying, recording, or information storage and retrieval without permission in writing from the publisher.

Please see photo credits for image license information.

ISBN: 978-0-9860427-1-3

Designed in Florida
United States of America

Printed in China

SiestaKeyBook.com
Stooksbury@HigherLevelPublishing.com

Higher Level Publishing
1001 Riverside Dr. (Suite 240)
Palmetto, FL 34221

Higher Level Publishing

HigherLevelPublishing.com

SIESTA KEY

THE BOOK

By Danny Stooksbury

TABLE OF CONTENTS

Siesta Key People & Places
    Aerial Photo Spread Of Siesta Key .... 2 & 3
    Beach Photo Spread .... 4 & 5
    Siesta Beach Lifeguard Stand Photo Spread .... 6 & 7
    Sarasota Key 8
    20th Century 9
    Magical Sand 10
    Day & Night 11
    Shallow Water Photo 12
    Island Love 13
    Key To Explore 14
    Siesta's Fiestas 15
    City of Sarasota 16
    Embrace of Art 17
    Island Motion 18
    Sarasota Bay 19
    Siesta Beach 20
    Turtle Beach 21
    Crescent Beach 22
    Siesta Sunsets 23

Siesta Key Animals & Vegetation
    Beach Blossom 24
    Sand Dunes 25
    State Symbols 26
    Florida Oranges 27
    Brown Pelican Photo 28
    Brown Pelicans 29
    Birds At Sea 30
    Finite Flock 31
    White Birds 32
    Fancy Feathers 33
    Sea Photo 34
    Sea Hawks 35
    Sea Grass 36
    Sea Life 37
    Wild Dolphins 38
    Bottlenose Dolphin Photo 39
    Rockin' Reptiles 40
    Life In Shells 41
    Life Aquatic 42
    Stunning Sprouts 43
    Florida Beach Photo Spread .... 44 & 45
    Sea Gulls Photo Spread .... 46 & 47
    Manatee Photo Spread .... 48 & 49
    Green Sea Turtle Photo Spread .... 50 & 51

Photo Credits 53
Sources & Recommended Reading / Information Centers 55
Index 56

Siesta Key is a barrier island on Florida's west coast. It was virtually uninhabited prior to the twentieth century and was only accessible by boat. Because of its proximity to Sarasota, it was once known as Sarasota Key. Its dense vegetation and dangerous wildlife made Sarasota Key unfit for tourists.

ABOVE: This aerial photograph, taken in 1951, looks north across Siesta Key. Some of the early stages of development on the island are evident, including simple roads and small structures.

SARASOTA KEY

Sarasota Key was rebranded Siesta Key in 1917 in an attempt to help attract tourists. The development of accommodations, restaurants, and shopping centers has lured millions of people to the three-and-a-half-square-mile island.

TOP LEFT: Workers constructing a home on Siesta Key in the early 1950s.

TOP RIGHT: Visitors relax poolside in 1954 in the Sarasota-by-the-Sea subdivision.

BOTTOM: This aerial photograph, taken in 1979, shows Siesta Key's development.

Siesta Key boasts sugar-white sand composed almost entirely of eroded quartz rock once found in the Appalachian Mountains.

MAGICAL SAND

TOP: Siesta Beach, with its soft, powdery sand, is regularly rated among the top beaches in America.

BOTTOM LEFT: The brilliant white shade is easily seen in these magnified quartz sand rocks.

BOTTOM RIGHT: A handful of Siesta Beach sand demonstrates its fine quality.

Siesta Key's warm tropical environment is enjoyed by more than one million visitors every year. Big, blue skies and colorful sunsets make every day worth savoring.

TOP LEFT: Lightning strikes off the Florida Gulf Coast, one of the world's most active locations for lightning.

TOP RIGHT: The sun and clouds paint a beautiful scene on Siesta Beach.

BOTTOM: Siesta Key beachgoers enjoy as many as 350 days of sunshine each year.

DAY & NIGHT

11

Romance and Siesta Key go hand in hand. Tens of thousands of love birds flock to Siesta Key's beaches every year.

PREVIOUS PAGE: The union of sand and sea on Siesta Key sets the scene for love.

TOP LEFT: It's all too easy to fall in love on the beaches of Siesta Key.

TOP RIGHT: Thousands of people are married on Siesta Key each year.

BOTTOM: A family shares a beach stroll.

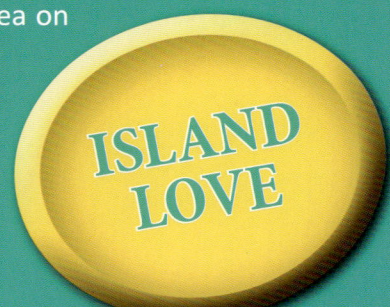

ISLAND LOVE

Siesta Key has endless opportunities for exploration. Adventurers enjoy its constantly evolving beaches and numerous nature trails, as well as the Gulf and other bodies of water.

KEY TO EXPLORE

TOP: Paddleboarding has rapidly become a favorite method of exploring the water around Siesta Key.

BOTTOM LEFT: Children playing on Siesta Beach build a sandcastle.

BOTTOM RIGHT: Shelling is a fun form of treasure hunting on Siesta Key's beaches.

Siesta Key visitors and residents enjoy the island's active nightlife and frequent beach festivities, including a weekly drum circle that begins an hour before sunset each Sunday.

TOP LEFT: The Crystal Classic is a popular sand sculpting event held each fall.

BOTTOM LEFT: Sign welcoming visitors to Siesta Key Village, the island's epicenter for shopping, dining, and nightlife.

RIGHT: A fire dancer performs at a Siesta Key drum circle on Siesta Beach.

SIESTA'S FIESTAS

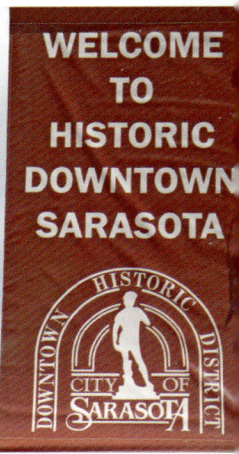

Siesta Key's close proximity to Sarasota allows residents and guests to enjoy the relaxed beach atmosphere and big-city entertainment. Fittingly, Sarasota's city motto is "Where Urban Amenities Meet Small-Town Living."

TOP SPREAD: Sarasota's downtown skyline.

BOTTOM LEFT: Dolphin fountain found downtown in Sarasota's Bayfront Park.

BOTTOM RIGHT: Downtown Sarasota street banner showing a city symbol, which includes the Michelangelo statue "David."

CITY OF SARASOTA

Sarasota embraces many forms of artistic expression. Some of the most iconic displays are the numerous sculptures that have become a major component of the eclectic cityscape.

BOTTOM LEFT: This twenty-five-foot statue, "Unconditional Surrender" by John Seward Johnson II, stands in downtown Sarasota on US Highway 41.

BOTTOM RIGHT: This replica of the "Fountain of Oceanus" is one of more than ten thousand pieces of art located at the John and Mable Ringling Museum of Art.

EMBRACE OF ART

From bicycles, Segways, and scooters to paddleboards, speed boats, Jet Skis, and more, there are lots of ways to keep yourself moving on and around Siesta Key.

TOP: Siesta Key's North Bridge. A 2010 survey found an average of seventeen thousand vehicles cross this bridge each day.

BOTTOM LEFT: Street signs found at the corner of Beach Road and Ocean Boulevard.

BOTTOM: Powerboats are piled high at this Siesta Key marina.

Sarasota Bay is a 150-square-mile estuary located along the western coast of central Florida. The bay divides Siesta Key and the state's mainland, as well as other barrier islands, including Lido Key, Longboat Key, and Casey Key.

TOP: The Ringling Bridge, located adjacent to Siesta Key, crosses Sarasota Bay to Lido Key. The bridge is easily seen from the north shores of Siesta Key.

BOTTOM: Anchored vessels resting in the Sarasota Bay waters between Siesta Key and Sarasota.

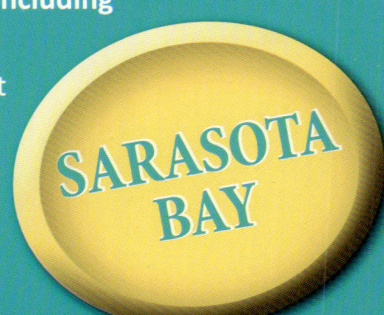

Siesta Beach was named "America's Best Beach 2011" by Dr. Stephen Leatherman, a beach expert and the author of the blog "Dr. Beach." It is one of many awards won by Siesta Beach, which has the purest quartz sand in the world.

TOP: Yellow, red, blue, and green lifeguard stands add color to the white, powdery sand on Siesta Beach. The lifeguards and shallow waters keep this beach safe.

BOTTOM: A Siesta Beach sign located on Beach Drive welcomes visitors to one of the top beaches in the world.

Turtle Beach is located in the southern region of Siesta Key. Its sand is primarily composed of a mixture of quartz and shells. Turtle Beach has boat ramps, a playground, and a covered picnic area.

TOP LEFT: Blind Pass Lagoon is located in Turtle Beach Park. It is a popular launch spot for kayakers and boaters.

TOP RIGHT: Turtle Beach is a popular location for beach fishing.

BOTTOM: This sign welcomes visitors at the entrance of Turtle Beach Park.

TURTLE BEACH

21

Cresent Beach is the most clandestine public beach on Siesta Key. It is located just south of Siesta Beach. What it lacks in amenities, Crescent Beach makes up for with a quiet atmosphere that makes it a favorite destination for people happy to escape the crowds.

CRESCENT BEACH

TOP: From the southern end of Crescent Beach, you can see the bow shape formed by Siesta Beach and Crescent Beach.

BOTTOM: Point of Rocks, accessible from Crescent Beach, is a collection of rocks where visitors come to spot sea life at low tide.

Siesta Key sunsets are full of magic. When the sun reaches the Gulf horizon, its light passes through the air above the water, allowing small molecules and salt particles to scatter the sun's light rays. All of the blue and violet colors are refracted away. Meanwhile, beautiful rays of reds and yellows are left to paint the Siesta Key sky.

ABOVE: Siesta Key occupies eight miles of western coastline from which to watch the sun set. The warm Gulf water, white-sand beaches, and wide-open skies make the sunsets seen from Siesta Key unique.

SIESTA SUNSETS

Siesta Key has large amounts of sand and salt, and constantly faces erosion and changing sea levels. These conditions may seem harsh, but some plant species thrive here.

BEACH BLOSSOM

TOP: Mangrove trees have remarkable root systems that wildly overlap to latch on to and stabilize loose soil and sand.

BOTTOM LEFT: Beach sunflowers have a special ability to survive in very salty soil.

BOTTOM RIGHT: Sea grape trees on Siesta Key's beaches produce these grape-like fruits.

The naturally forming dunes found on Siesta Key's beaches are called "foredunes" or "beach ridges." They are formed by windblown sand and stabilized by the roots of natural vegetation.

TOP: You can distinguish the age of a dune by the types of vegetation on it. Grasses can take root in a matter of weeks, while shrubs may take decades to develop.

BOTTOM: Sea oats thrive in the loose, salty sand found on Siesta Key beaches. The beautiful long stalks withstand high winds, while their roots prevent erosion.

SAND DUNES

Florida has many state symbols, which include animals, flowers, flags, and more. Here are a few you might be lucky enough to spot on or around Siesta Key.

STATE SYMBOLS

TOP: Manatees are Florida's official state freshwater marine mammals.

BOTTOM LEFT: The orange blossom was named the state flower of Florida in 1909.

BOTTOM RIGHT: Siesta Key is often visited by Florida's state bird, the mockingbird.

Orange is more than just Florida's most famous fruit!

TOP LEFT: The orange lily is popular among Florida gardeners.

BOTTOM LEFT: This state has more than 50 million citrus trees according to the Florida Department of Agriculture.

RIGHT: The Gulf fritillary, or passion butterfly, has a brilliant orange color. The species is native to Florida's Gulf Coast.

FLORIDA ORANGES

Brown pelicans, known for their distinct throat pouches, have found their very own paradise in the shallow waters of Siesta Key.

PREVIOUS PAGE: This mature brown pelican offers a glimpse of its webbed feet. The webbing helps with paddling in the water.

TOP: Brown pelicans nest in colonies and can be observed hunting in groups.

BOTTOM: Brown pelicans have wingspans in the range of six to eight feet.

BROWN PELICANS

Birds are as common to the Gulf's seashore as fish are to the water. Siesta Key's waterbirds come in all sizes, from very small sandpipers to very tall great blue herons.

BIRDS AT SEA

TOP: Sandpipers utilize the ocean surf to locate and eat small bugs and crustaceans by pecking into the loose sand.

BOTTOM: Great blue herons shadow Siesta Key fishers in anticipation of scraps. When full grown, they stand at nearly five feet tall and have a wingspan of more than six feet.

There are many endangered animals found on Siesta Key or in the surrounding waters. Here are some rare birds seen on Siesta Key.

LEFT: Wood storks live year-round on Siesta Key. They nest in pairs, and there are as few as five thousand nests left in North America.

TOP RIGHT: Cape Sable seaside sparrows are thirteen-inch nonmigratory birds.

BOTTOM RIGHT: Swallow-tailed kites build nests in trees near water.

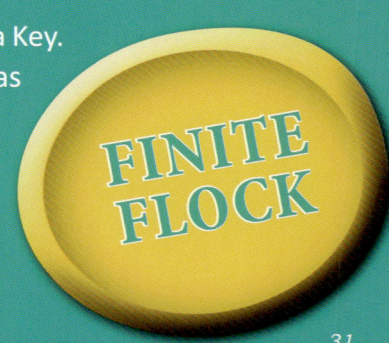

FINITE FLOCK

Siesta Key is home to many beautiful creatures, but the ones that best reflect the island's unsullied spirit are the white birds.

TOP & BOTTOM LEFT: White ibis use their long curved beaks to dig up crabs and insects, or, if they're lucky enough, to catch fish.

TOP RIGHT: A fully grown great egret can have a wingspan of almost five feet.

BOTTOM RIGHT: Snowy egrets look similar to great egrets but can be distinguished by their black beaks and golden feet.

WHITE BIRDS

Most feathers serve critical functions such as flying or providing birds with warmth, but some feathers also provide a little flare.

TOP: If you find a pink feather on Siesta Key, it's likely from a roseate spoonbill. These beautiful birds have pink and white plumage, orange tail feathers, and red legs.

BOTTOM: Wild black-hooded parakeets are often spotted flying in the skies of Sarasota County. Parakeets have become abundant in southern Florida after many pet birds escaped or were set free.

FANCY FEATHERS

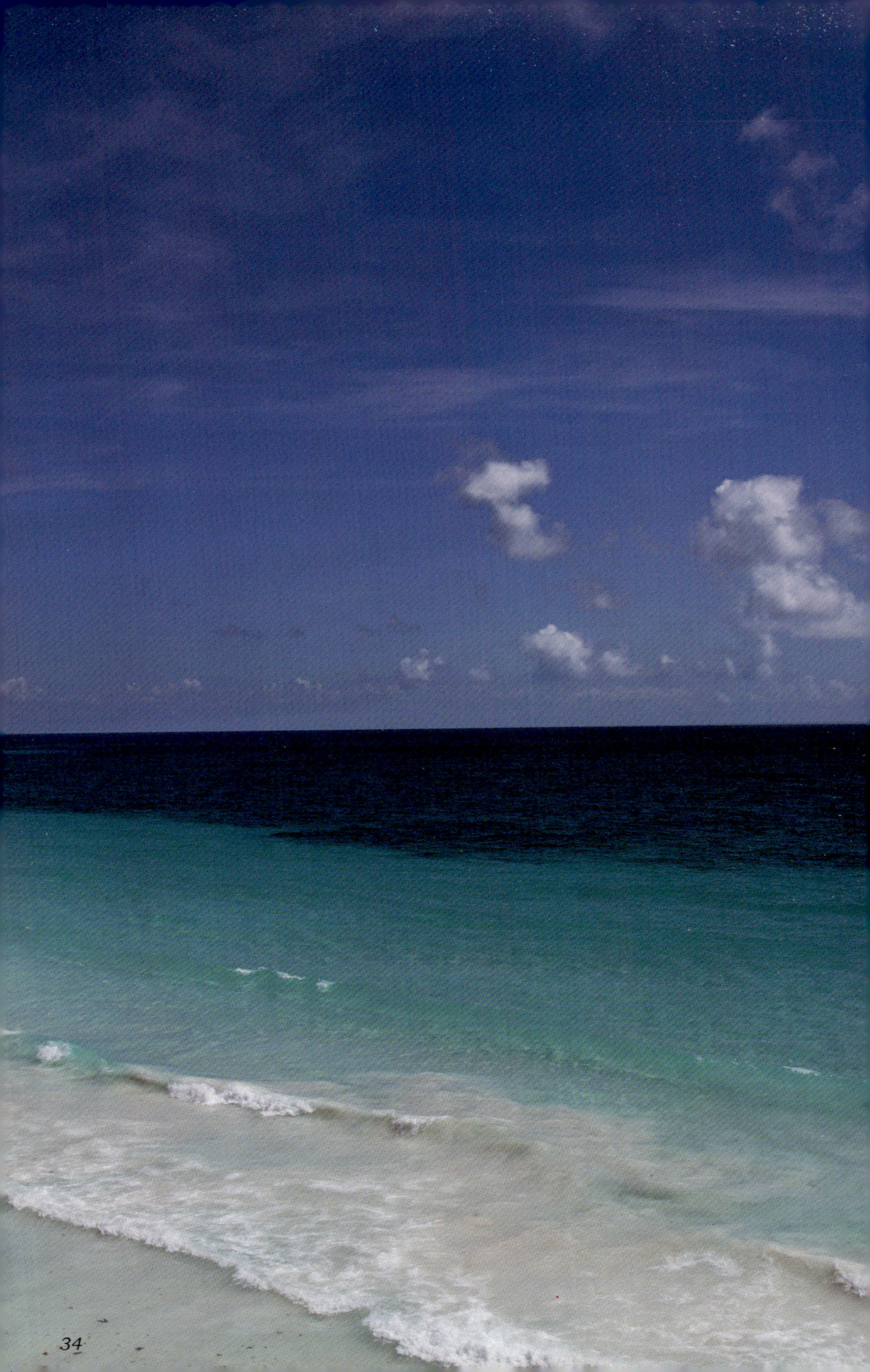

Siesta Key is a common nesting location for ospreys, also known as sea hawks.

TOP: Sea hawks get their nickname from their incredible ability to snatch fish by plunging their talons into the water.

BOTTOM LEFT: Ospreys are easy to distinguish thanks to the masking brown stripes across their faces.

BOTTOM RIGHT: Full-grown ospreys have a wingspan of four to five feet.

SEA HAWKS

Florida waterways contain around 2.2 million acres of sea grasses, which are vital to the natural habitat. Sea grasses maintain water clarity. They provide shelter for small fish, crustaceans, and shellfish. The grasses also serve as food for numerous animals. Plus, their roots stabilize the ground.

SEA GRASS

ABOVE: Manatee grass grows to around twenty inches. It is a preferred meal of manatees. There are many areas where manatee grass grows in the waters around Siesta Key.

The Gulf of Mexico is the ninth-largest body of water in the world at approximately 600,000 square miles. Deep within its waters are some of nature's most incredible creatures.

TOP LEFT: Blue marlin found in the Gulf can weigh more than one thousand pounds.

TOP RIGHT: Spotted eagle rays grow to eight feet long and ten feet wide.

BOTTOM: The Gulf contains some shark species, including scalloped hammerheads, as seen in this picture.

SEA LIFE

Dolphin spotting is a popular Siesta Key pastime. Experts estimate there are approximately five thousand bottlenose dolphins that live in the waters surrounding the Sarasota region.

WILD DOLPHINS

TOP: Bottlenose dolphins live up to fifty years and grow to more than thirteen feet long.

BOTTOM: Bottlenose dolphins swim at speeds of up to eighteen miles per hour.

NEXT PAGE: Bottlenose dolphins can hold their breath underwater for twelve minutes.

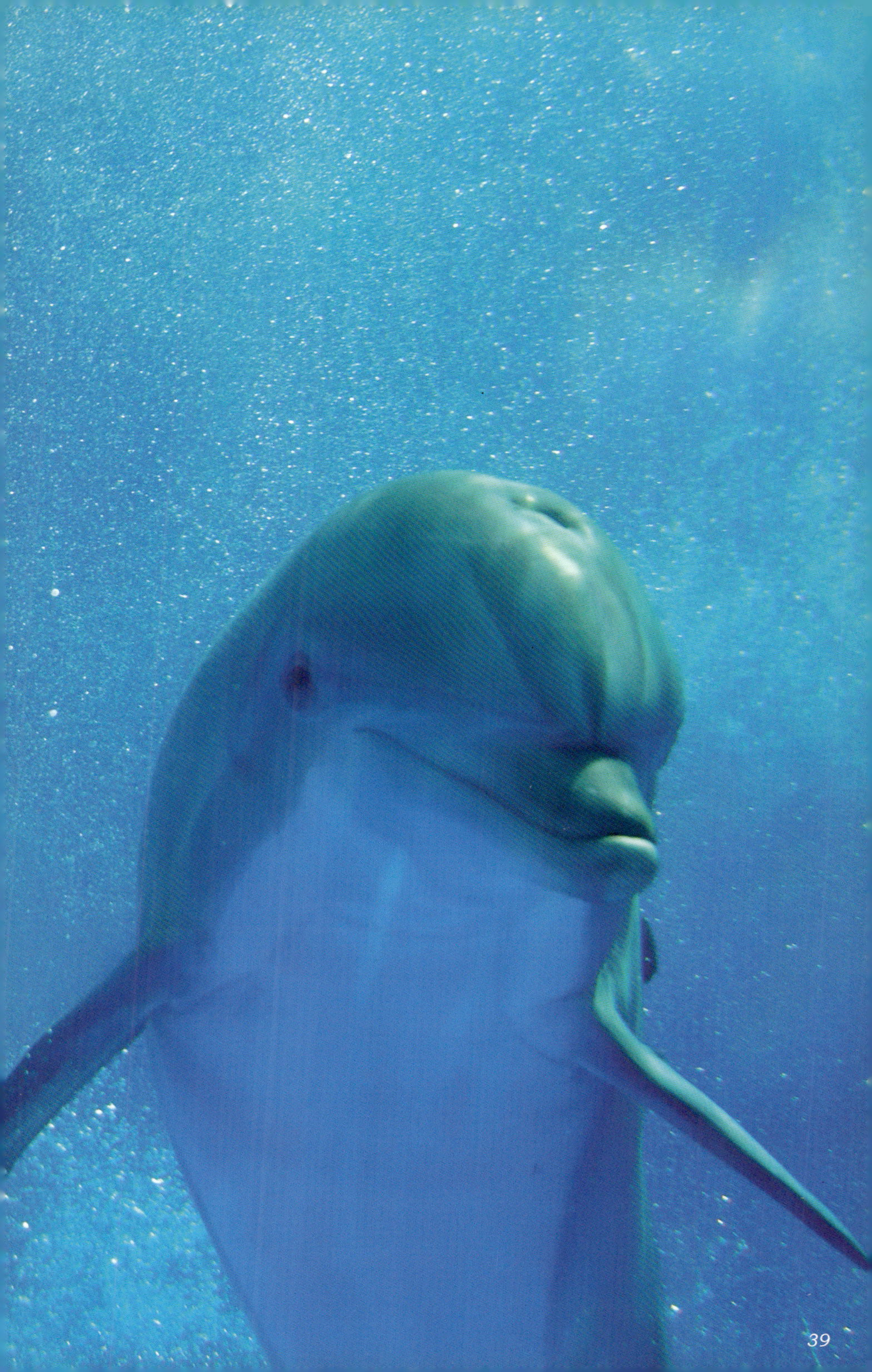

Florida's warm climate and numerous waterways make it an ideal habitat for many incredibly cool reptiles.

TOP: Florida's state reptile, the alligator, can grow to fourteen feet long.

BOTTOM LEFT: Green sea turtle nests on Siesta Key can hold hundreds of hatchlings.

BOTTOM RIGHT: Geckos and other lizards are frequently found preying on insects in residential areas in Florida.

ROCKIN' REPTILES

Siesta Key has many shelled species. Here are a few shelled creatures that demonstrate the vast contrast in shell sizes.

TOP LEFT: Loggerhead sea turtles' shells grow to more than three and a half feet long.

TOP RIGHT: Florida crown conch shells easily fit in the palm of your hand.

BOTTOM: Fiddler crabs are very small and will leave their old shells behind when they outgrow them. A grown fiddler crab's shell is only about two inches long.

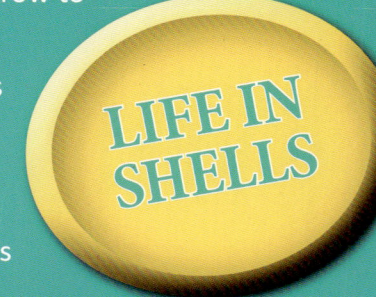

LIFE IN SHELLS

There is an astonishing amount of life in the waters on and around Siesta Key. Fish may dominate the sea, but other forms of life call the water home, too.

LIFE AQUATIC

TOP: Cormorants differ from other seabirds because their feathers are less buoyant, allowing them to swim well underwater.

BOTTOM LEFT: Water lilies blossom atop Siesta Key's inland waterways.

BOTTOM RIGHT: Atlantic spade fish hide along the coast of Siesta Key.

Siesta Key's moist climate, with constant sunshine and short periods of rainfall, makes for perfect conditions for growth of many beautiful plant varieties.

TOP: Purple passion flowers blossom from native vines along the Gulf Coast.

BOTTOM LEFT: Sarasota County is one of the rare Florida locations where summer torches are confirmed to grow naturally.

BOTTOM RIGHT: Aloe plants enjoy lots of sunlight and sandy soil.

STUNNING SPROUTS

43

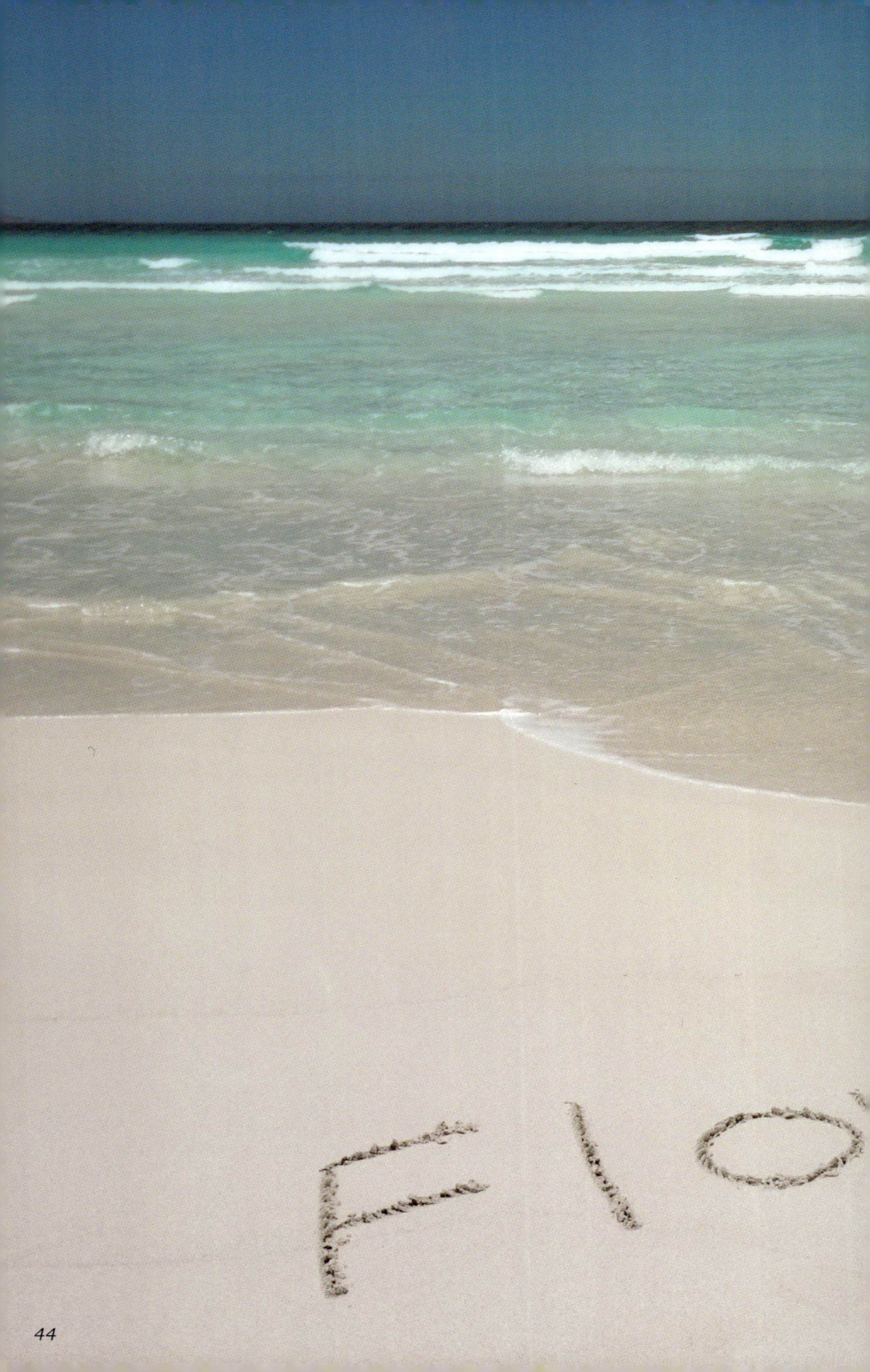

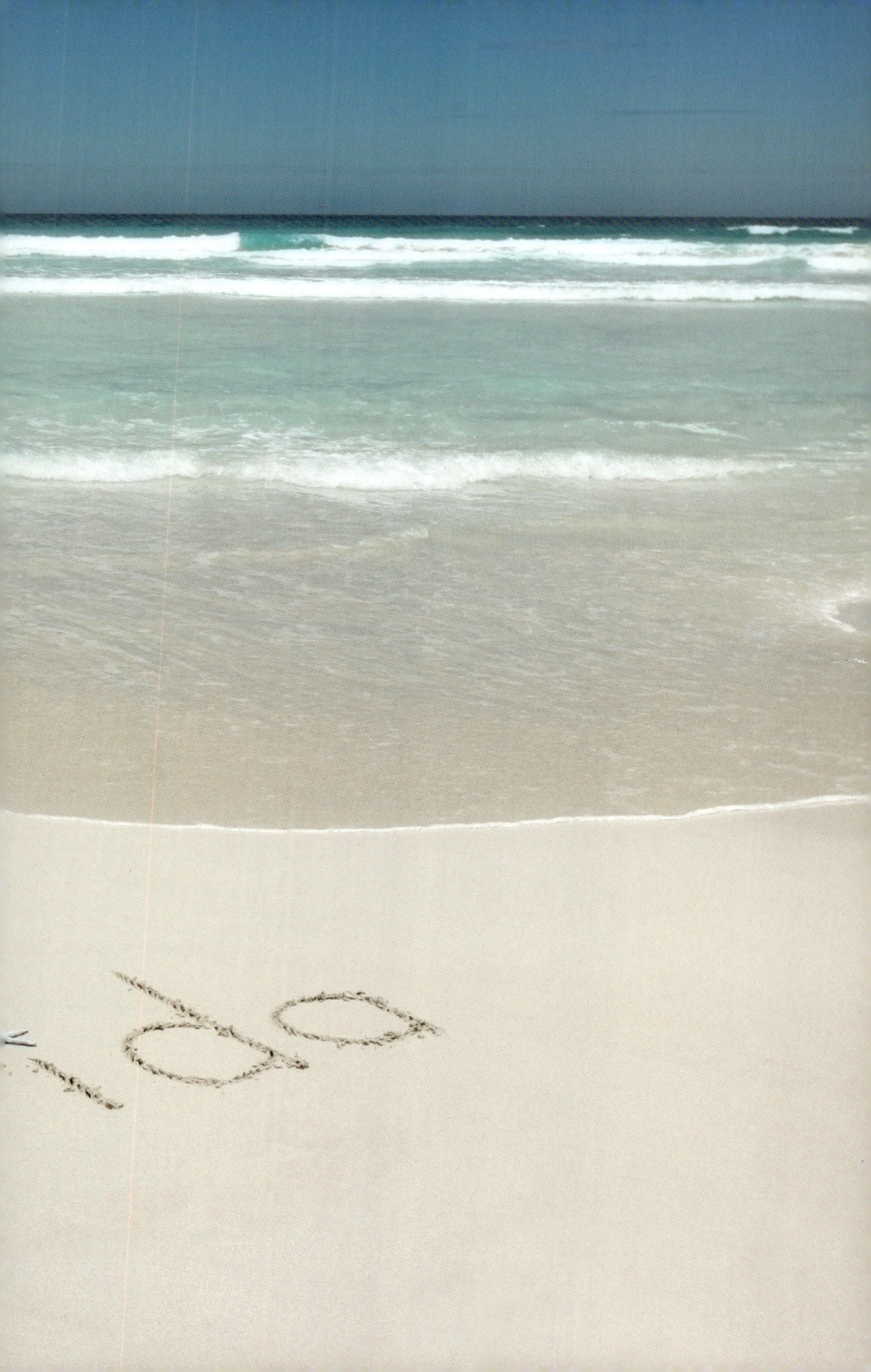

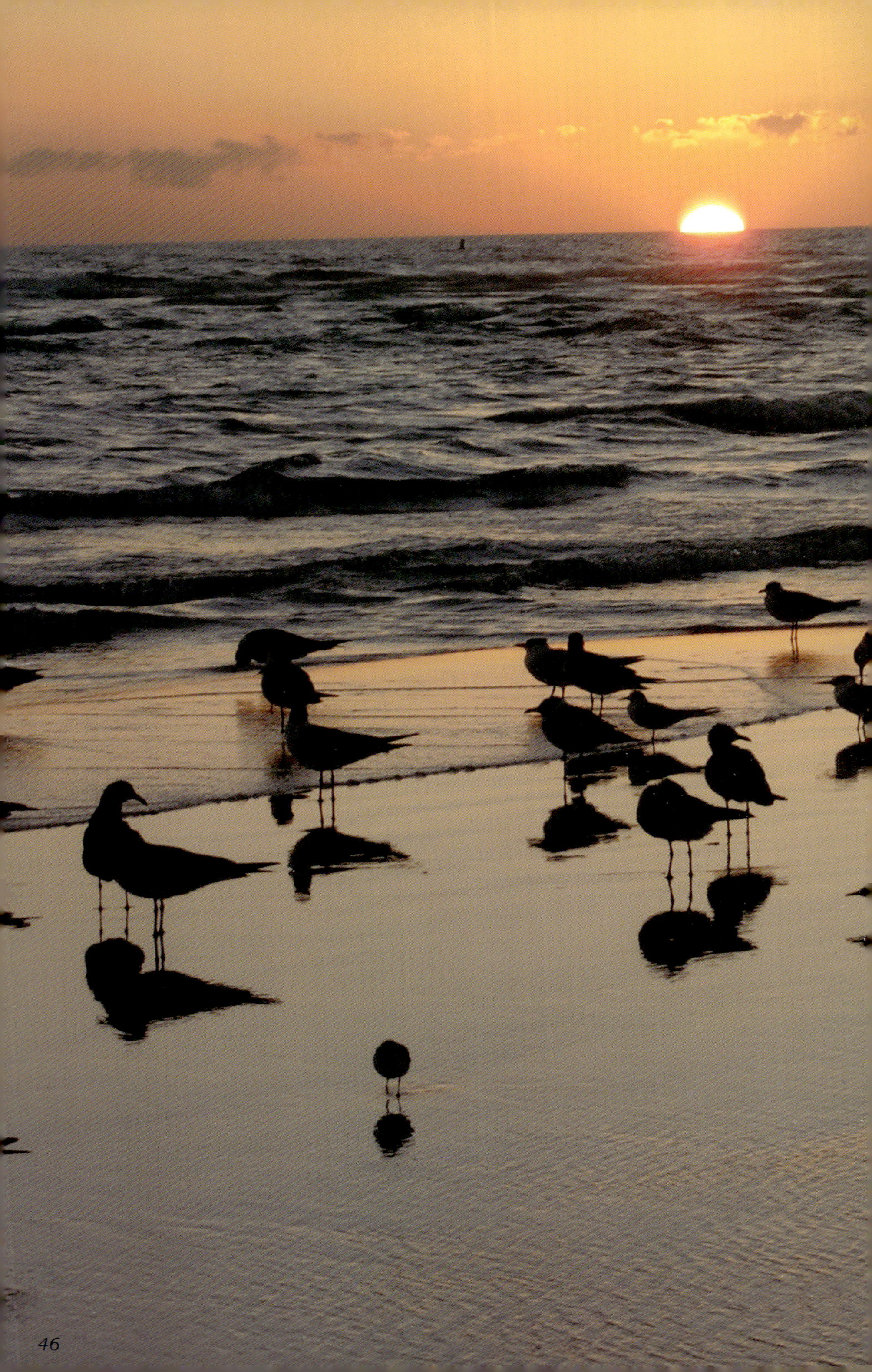

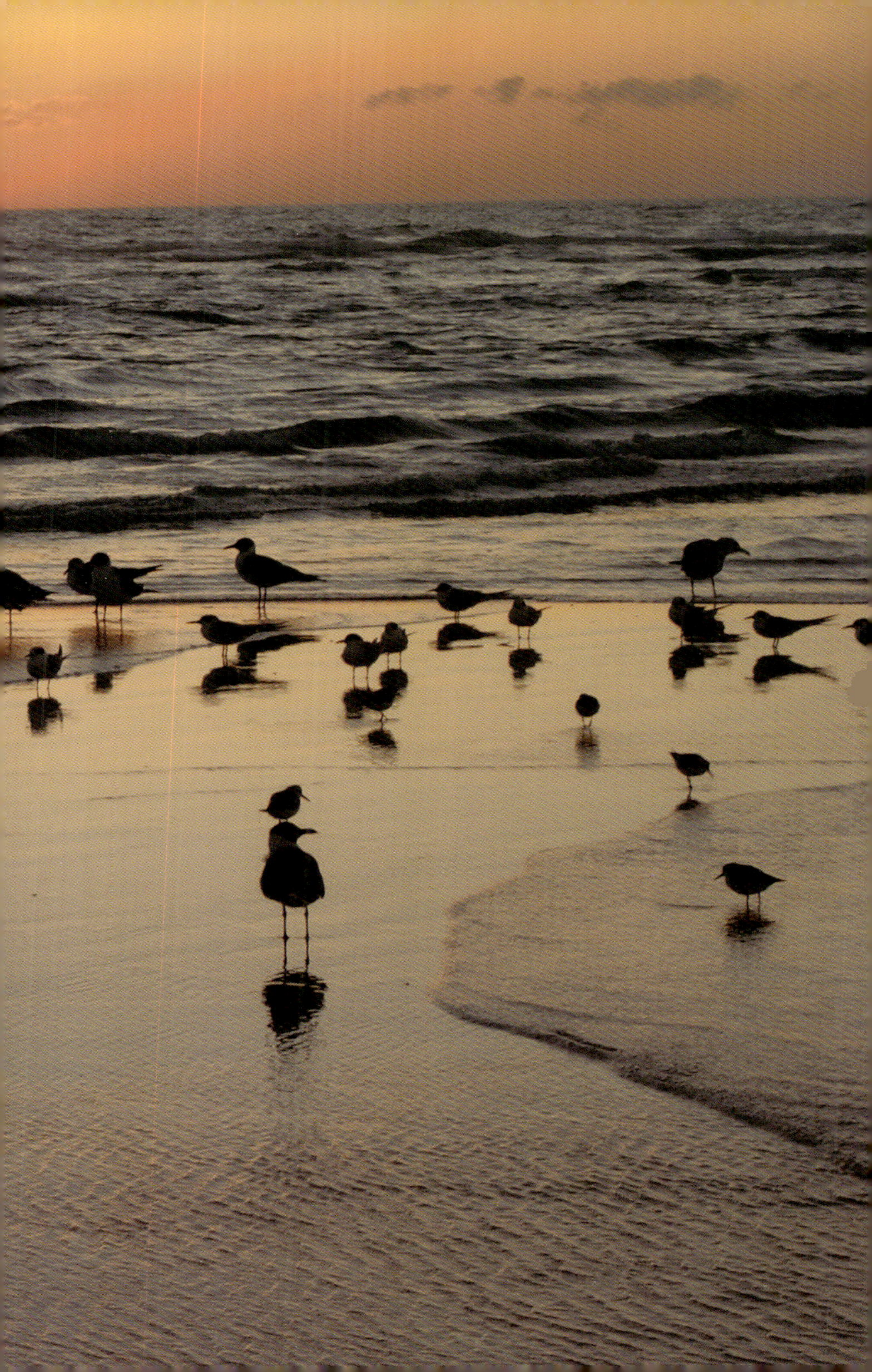

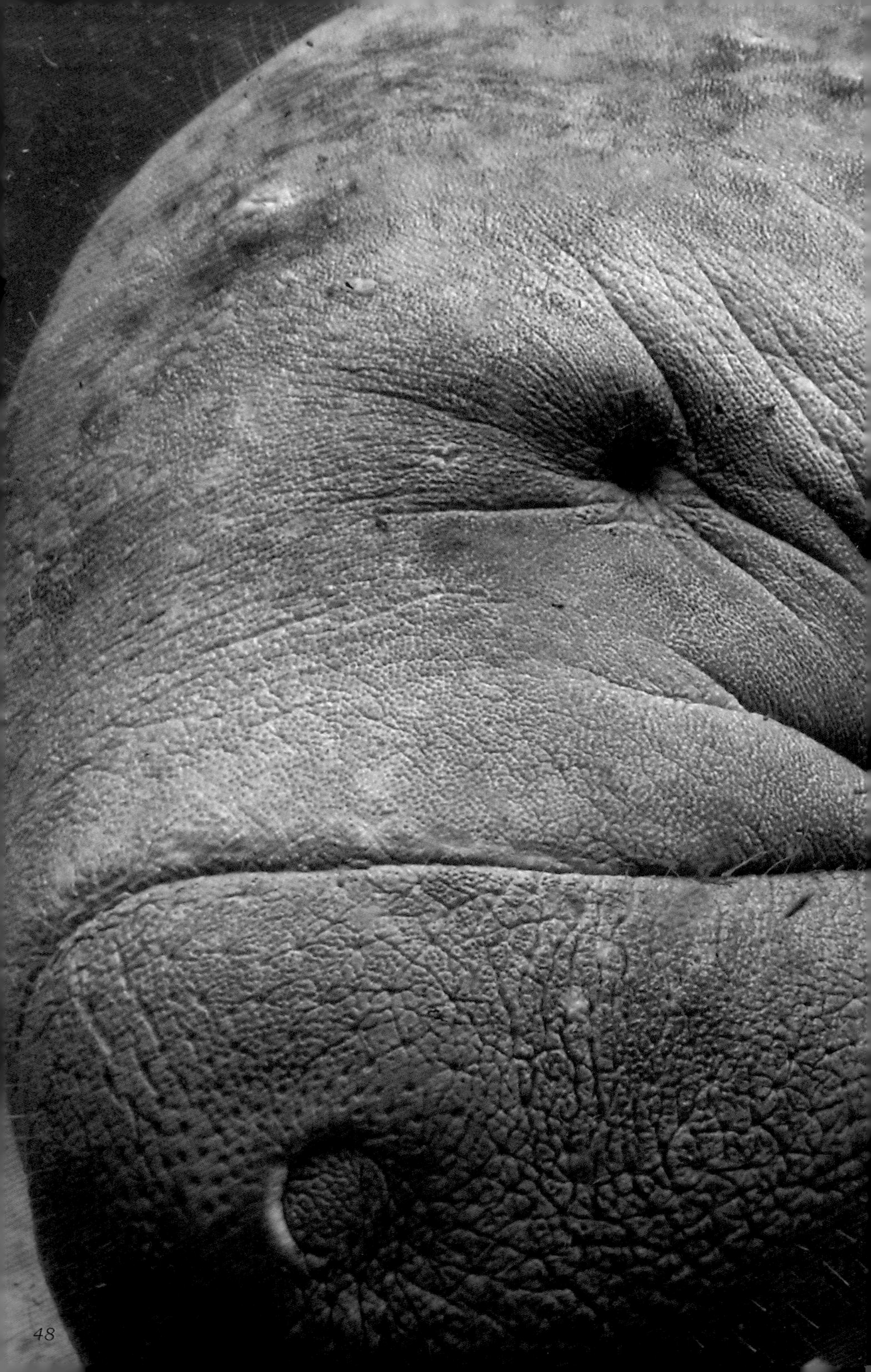

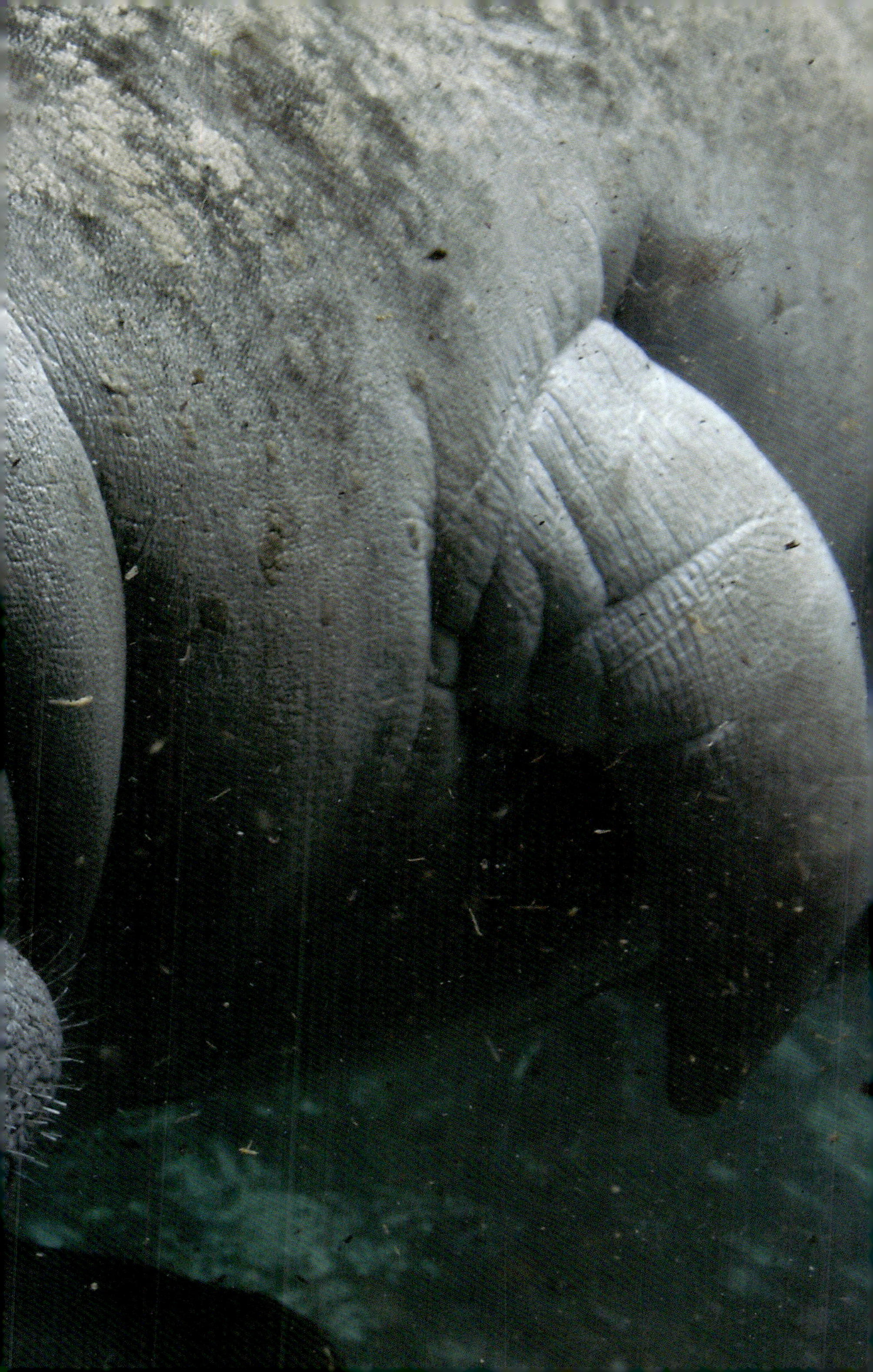

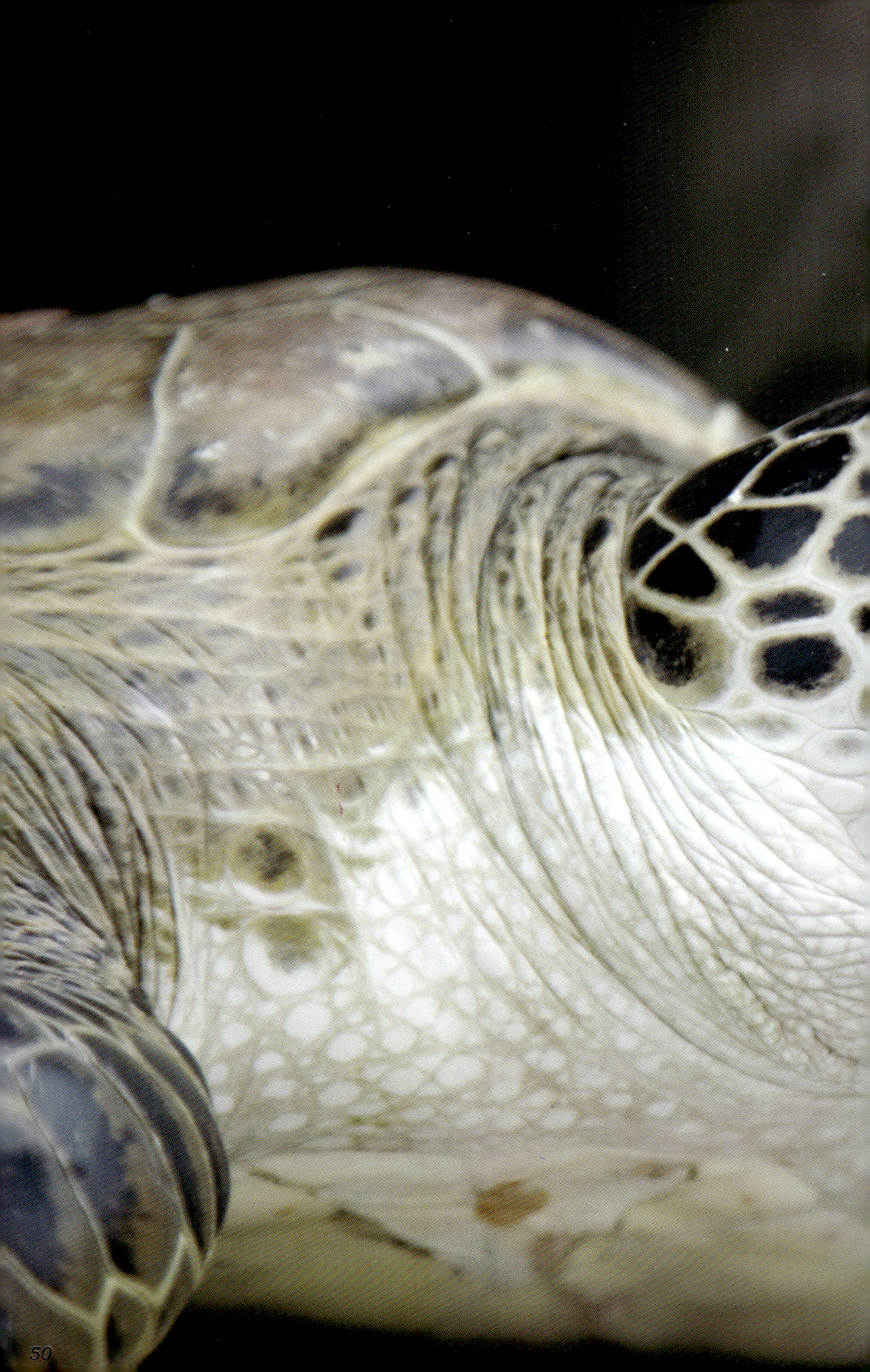

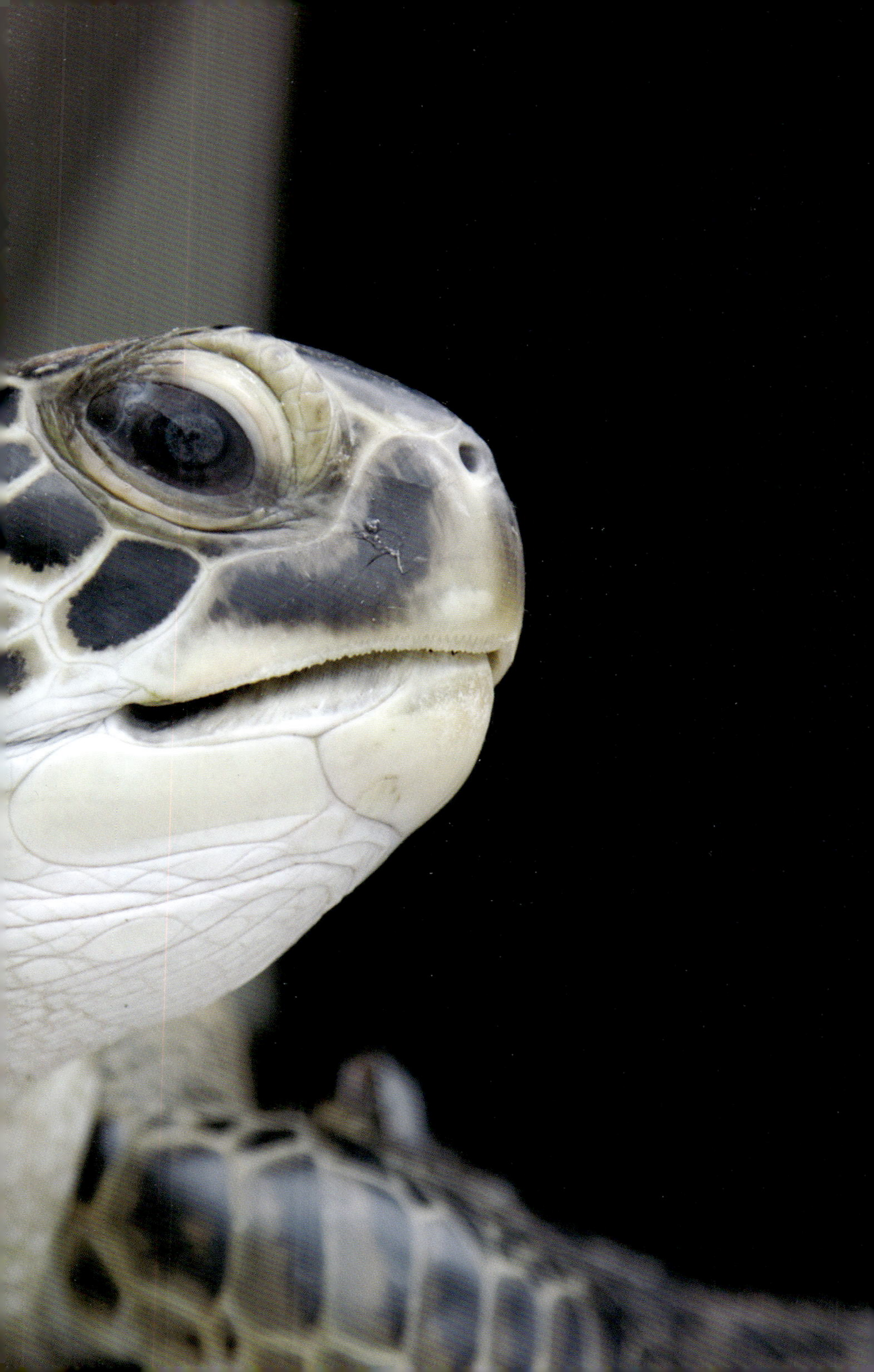

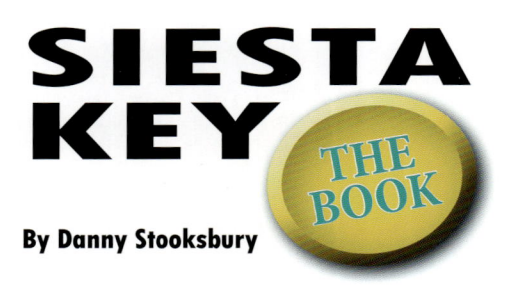

SIESTA KEY

THE BOOK

By Danny Stooksbury

PHOTOGRAPH CREDITS

A special thank you is owed to the very skilled photographers who made this project possible.

COVER & INTERIOR — Layout and design by Stooksbury, Danny.

PAGES 2 & 3 — SPREAD: LoftyLens Aerial Photography

PAGES 4 & 5 — SPREAD: Motmel. GNU

PAGES 6 & 7 — SPREAD: Bigstock

PAGE 8 — FULL PAGE: State Archives of Florida, Florida Memory: Joseph Janney Steinmetz

PAGE 9 — TOP LEFT: State Archives of Florida, Florida Memory: Joseph Janney Steinmetz; TOP RIGHT: State Archives of Florida, Florida Memory: Joseph Janney Steinmetz; BOTTOM: Tichnor Bros Inc. vintage postcard

PAGE 10 — TOP: iStock. 2013; BOTTOM LEFT: Public Domain. CC0; BOTTOM RIGHT: Robinson, Linda

PAGE 11 — TOP LEFT: Stooksbury, Danny; TOP RIGHT: Starr, Forest & Starr, Kim. CC BY; BOTTOM: Bigstock

PAGE 12 — FULL PAGE: iStock

PAGE 13 — TOP LEFT: Bigstock; TOP RIGHT: Bigstock; BOTTOM: Bigstock

PAGE 14 — TOP: Bigstock; BOTTOM LEFT: Bigstock; BOTTOM RIGHT: Bigstock

PAGE 15 — TOP LEFT: Bigstock; RIGHT: Bigstock; BOTTOM LEFT: Stooksbury, Danny

PAGE 16 — TOP: Bigstock; BOTTOM LEFT: Bigstock; BOTTOM RIGHT: Bigstock

PAGE 17 — TOP: Bigstock; BOTTOM LEFT: Bigstock; BOTTOM RIGHT: Bigstock

PAGE 18 — TOP: Bigstock; BOTTOM LEFT: Robinson, Linda; BOTTOM RIGHT: Bigstock

PAGE 19 — TOP: Bigstock; BOTTOM LEFT: Bigstock

PAGE 20 — TOP: iStock; BOTTOM: Stooksbury, Danny

PAGE 21 — TOP LEFT: Robinson, Linda; TOP RIGHT: Robinson, Linda; BOTTOM: Stooksbury, Danny

PAGE 22 — TOP: Stooksbury, Danny; BOTTOM: Stooksbury, Danny

PAGE 23 — TOP: Bigstock

PAGE 24 — TOP: Stooksbury, Danny; BOTTOM LEFT: Stooksbury, Danny; BOTTOM RIGHT: Stooksbury, Danny

PAGE 25 — TOP: Robinson, Linda; BOTTOM: Robinson, Linda

PAGE 26 — TOP: Bigstock; BOTTOM LEFT: Public Domain. CC0; BOTTOM RIGHT: Robinson, Linda

PAGE 27 — TOP LEFT: Public Domain. CC0; TOP RIGHT: Public Domain. CC0; BOTTOM LEFT: Bigstock

PAGE 28 — FULL PAGE: Robinson, Linda

PAGE 29 — TOP: Robinson, Linda; BOTTOM: Robinson, Linda

PAGE 30 — TOP: Robinson, Linda; BOTTOM: Stooksbury, Danny

PAGE 31 — LEFT: Karatay, Mehmet. CC BY SA; TOP RIGHT: Public Domain. CC0; BOTTOM RIGHT: Bigstock

PAGE 32 — TOP LEFT: Majorros, William H. CC BY-SA; TOP RIGHT: Public Domain. CC0; BOTTOM LEFT: Stooksbury, Danny; BOTTOM RIGHT: Stieglitz, Hans. CC BY-SA

PAGE 33 — TOP: Bigstock; BOTTOM: Apix *CC BY-SA*

PAGE 34 — FULL PAGE: Bigstock

PAGE 35 — TOP: Public Domain. CC0; BOTTOM LEFT: Carrasco, Simon. CC BY-SA; BOTTOM: Public Domain. CC0

PAGE 36 — TOP: Public Domain. CC0

PAGE 37 — TOP LEFT: Public Domain. CC0; TOP RIGHT: Public Domain. CC0 BOTTOM: Public Domain. CC0

PAGE 38 — TOP: Robinson, Linda; BOTTOM: Public Domain. CC0

PAGE 39 — FULL PAGE: Bigstock

PAGE 40 — TOP: Bigstock; BOTTOM: Bigstock; LOOSE: Bigstock

PAGE 41 — TOP LEFT: Public Domain. CC0; TOP RIGHT: Kathy. CC BY-SA; BOTTOM: Wood, Gary J. CC BY-SA

PAGE 42 — TOP: Public Domain. CC0; BOTTOM LEFT: Hoelscher, Matthew. CC BY-SA BOTTOM RIGHT: Bigstock

PAGE 43 — TOP: Bigstock; BOTTOM LEFT: Enders, Melissa. 2013; BOTTOM RIGHT: Bigstock

PAGES 44 & 45 — SPREAD: Bigstock

PAGES 46 & 47 — SPREAD: Motmel. CC BY-SA

PAGES 48 & 49 — SPREAD: Bigstock

PAGES 50 & 51 — SPREAD: Public Domain

GNU Free Documentation License — GNU
Creative Commons Attribution-ShareAlike — CC BY-SA
Creative Commons Attribution — CC BY
Public Domain – CC0

SOURCES & RECOMMENDED READING.

Kinser, Joshua Lawrence. Moon Handbooks: Florida Gulf Coast. Avalot Travel. 2011.

William R. Fontenot and Brian K. Miller. Birds of the Gulf Coast. Louisiana State University Press. 2001.

Sarasota History Center; 6062 Porter Way, Sarasota, FL, 34232

Sarasota History Center Museum; 701 N. Tamiami Trail; Sarasota, FL 34236

National Parks and Services: U.S. Department of Interior. NPS.gov.

St. Petersburg Times. Tampa Bay Through The Times. Seaside Publishing, Inc. 2008.

WEBSITES

Animals.Discovery.com

Animals.NationalGeographic.com.

BigStock.com

DrBeach.org

FoldingGuides.com.

iStock.com

VisitFlorida.org.

WhatBird.com.

USEFUL INFORMATION CENTERS

Siesta Key Chamber of Commerce
5118 Ocean Boulevard
Siesta Key, FL 34242

Siesta Key Visitor Information Center
1522 Stickney Point Road
Sarasota, Florida 34231

Sarasota History Center
6062 Porter Way,
Sarasota, FL 34232

Sarasota History Center Museum
701 N. Tamiami Trail
Sarasota, FL 34236

Florida Museum of Natural History
3215 Hull Rd.
Gainesville, FL 32611

Mote Aquarium
1600 Ken Thompson Pkwy.
Sarasota, FL 34236

South Florida Museum
201 10th St W.
Bradenton, FL 34205

INDEX

Here is an alphabetical list of names, places, and creatures found within this book with references to the pages on which they occur.

A

Alligator 40
America 10, 20, 22
Appalachian Mountains 10
ART 17
Atlantic spade fish 42

B

Bayfront Park 16
Beach Road 18
Beach sunflower 24
Bicycles 18
Blind Pass Lagoon 21
Bottlenose dolphin 38

C

Casey Key 19
Cape Sable seaside sparrow 31
Conch 41
Cormorant 42
Crescent Beach 22
Crustacean 30, 36
Crystal Classic 15

D

David 16
Dolphin 16, 38
Dr. Beach 20
Drum circle 15
Dune 26

E

Eagle ray 37
Egret 32

F

Fiddler crab 41
Florida 8, 11, 219, 26, 27, 33, 36, 40, 35, 37
Foredune 25
Fountain of Oceanus 17

G

Gecko 40

Grasses 36
Great blue herons 30
Green sea turtle 40
Gulf of Mexico 11, 14, 26, 27, 30, 37
Gulf fritillary 27

I

Ibis 32

J

Jet Ski 18
Johnson, John Seward II 17

L

Leatherman, Stephen 20
Lido Key 19
Lightning 11
Lilly 42
Loggerhead sea turtle 41
Longboat Key 19
Love 13

M

Manatee 26
Manatee grass 36
Mangrove tree 24
Marlin 37
Michelangelo 16
Mockingbird 26

N

North Bridge 18

O

Ocean Boulevard 18
Orange 27
Orange blossom 26
Osprey 35

P

Paddleboard 18
Parakeet 33
Passion flower 43
Pelican 29

Pink feather 33
Point of Rocks 22
Powerboat 18

R

Ringling Bridge 19
Ringling Museum of Art 17
Romance 13

S

Sand 10, 13, 15, 20, 21, 23, 24, 25
Sandcastle 14
Sandpiper 30
Sarasota Bay 19
Sarasota County 33, 43
Sarasota-by-the-Sea 9
Sarasota Key 8, 9
Scooter 18
Sea grape tree 24
Sea oat 25
Segway 18
Sea hawk 35
Shark 37
Shelling 14
Siesta Beach 10, 11, 14, 15, 20
Siesta Key 8, 9, 10, 11, 13, 14, 15, 16, 18, 19, 21, 23, 24, 25, 26, 29, 30, 31, 32, 33, 35, 36, 37, 40, 41, 42, 43
Siesta Key Village 15
Speed boat 18

T

Turtle Beach 21
Turtle Beach Park 21

U

Unconditional Surrender 17
US Highway 17, 35

W

Wood storks 31

To myself I am only a child playing on the beach, while vast oceans of truth lie undiscovered before me.

— *Isaac Newton*

HigherLevelPublishing.com